AIR POLLUTION

A TRUE BOOK

by

Rhonda Lucas Donald

Children's Press®
A Division of Scholastic Inc.

New York Toronto London Auckland Sydney
Mexico City New Delhi Hong Kong
Danbury, Connecticut

Pollution coming from smokestacks

Reading Consultant
Linda Cornwell
*Coordinator of School Quality
and Professional Improvement
Indiana State Teachers
Association*

Content Consultant
Jan Jenner
*Rendalia Biologist
Talladega, AL*

*Author's Dedication:
For Patrick*

Library of Congress Cataloging-in-Publication Data

Donald, Rhonda Lucas, 1962–
    Air pollution / by Rhonda Lucas Donald.
        p. cm. — (A true book)
    Includes bibliographical references and index.
    Summary: Explains what air pollution is, how it harms plants and ani-
mals, and how to help prevent it.
    ISBN 0-516-22191-4 (lib. bdg.)   0-516-25998-9 (pbk.)
    1. Air—Pollution—Juvenile literature. [1. Air—Pollution. 2. Pollution.]
I. Title. II. Series.
TD883.13 .D657 2001
363.739'2—dc21
                                    00-057041
                                          CIP
                                          AC

Contents

Volcanoes are a natural source of air pollution.

What Is That in the Air?

Soot. Smoke. Smog. When you think of air pollution, you probably think of one of these "S" words. Maybe you imagine a factory stack puffing out clouds of smoke. The truth is you cannot see many forms of air pollution. Anything that gets into the air and does not harmlessly vanish is air pollution. That includes smoke from fires, gases that come from burning fuel, and even dust.

Some air pollution is natural. Erupting volcanoes put out tons of smoke, ash, and gases. Forest fires create the same things as they burn. Strong winds can pick up and carry dirt and sand, creating dust storms that choke the air. In fact, air pollution may

Forest fires must be put out quickly to help keep the air clean.

have led to the extinction of the dinosaurs sixty-five million years ago. Some scientists think that a giant asteroid slammed into the Earth, sending tons of dirt and smoke high into the atmosphere. The thick dust completely blocked the sun's rays for months. Without the sun, the plants died, and without the plants, the dinosaurs could not survive.

People Pollution

"Natural" air pollution may cause big troubles, but things people do every day can be just as dangerous. Every time you ride in a car, switch on a light, or turn up the heat, you add to air pollution. How? The gas that runs your car, the coal that powers electricity

An everyday activity like watching TV adds to air pollution.

makers called generators, and
the oil or gas that heats your
home are all fossil fuels.
Burning fossil fuels releases
gases into the air—toxic or

Gasoline, oil heaters, and coal pollute the air when they are used.

poison gases. It also creates dust, soot, and tiny bits of stuff called particulates that pollute the air.

Some of the polluting gases, such as carbon monoxide, are very poisonous by themselves. Others cause trouble when they combine with other things in the air. For example, chemicals mix with water in the air to make acid. Eventually, the acidic water falls as rain— acid rain. Acid rain can also come down as snow or hang low to the ground as fog. No matter how it comes down,

Acid snow? Acid rain can also come down as snow, fog, sleet or hail.

Pedal power—bicycle riding is a good way to reduce pollution.

Natural ozone high in the Earth's atmosphere is a good thing. It acts like a sunscreen and filters out the sun's harmful rays, but ozone that forms at ground level is a type of air pollution. Sadly, the helpful ozone layer is also a victim of air pollution. Chemicals called CFCs that are used in refrigerators, air

Refrigerators have CFCs that can harm the ozone layer.

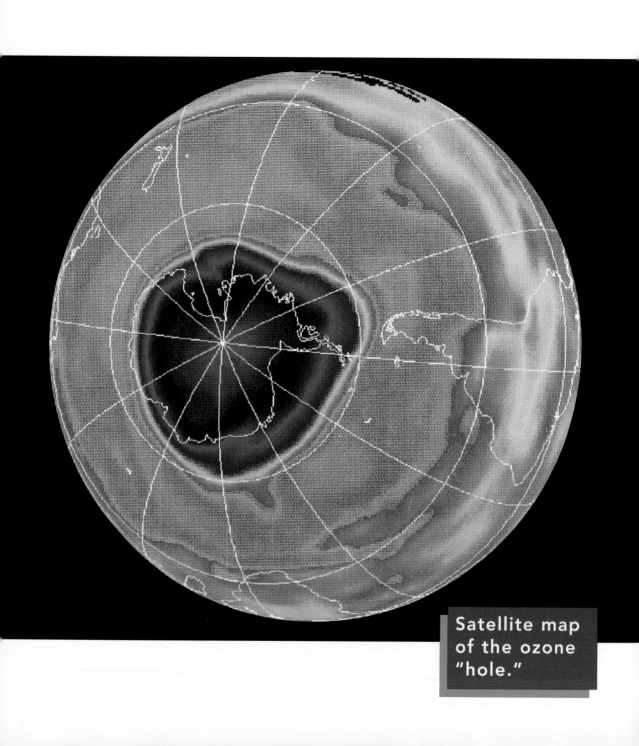

Satellite map of the ozone "hole."

conditioners, and some cleaners eat away at the ozone layer. That is why "holes" in the ozone layer exist above the north and south poles, where the super cold air causes the most ozone loss.

When pollutants get into the air, they can do far-reaching damage. Picked up by the wind, chemicals like those in pesticides cause trouble when they come down again with rain or snow and build up in bodies of water. Fish and other water creatures then eat the chemicals. The poisons build up in the animals' bodies over time. Predators that eat poisoned animals get a double dose of the toxins. DDT, a pesticide carried in the air, caused the near extinction of several species of birds of prey. The chemical caused the birds' eggshells to become thin and break, so the birds could not reproduce. Banning DDT in the United States

Peregrine falcons (above and being fed by human helper, right) were once endangered because of pollutants. Once the pesticide DDT was banned, peregrine falcons came back from near extinction.

helped bring the peregrine falcon and other species back from near extinction.

Make a Pollution Trap

Smear a thin layer of petroleum jelly on the inside of a white plastic lid. Set the lid outside, jelly-side up. Wait a day or two, and then check your trap. Can you identify any of the particles? Next set your trap inside for a day or two. Compare the level of outdoor pollution with what you find indoors. Can you think of ways to cut the indoor pollution?

Petroleum jelly
"Pollution Trap."

Pollution Problems

What we breathe goes into our lungs and bodies. Airborne pollutants can make breathing difficult and can even lead to diseases such as cancer. Carbon monoxide is so dangerous that a lot of it can cause death if breathed indoors. Smog interferes with

Cigarette smoke contains carbon monoxide, a poison gas.

people's breathing too, especially if they have lung disease, but it also burns people's eyes. Smog even causes rubber to wear out faster!

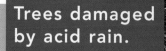

Trees damaged by acid rain.

You can see the effects of acid rain in the bare branches of high Appalachian Mountain trees. Worse still is what acid rain does to ponds and lakes.

Lake polluted by acid rain (above).
Acid rain is bad for fish.

The acid collects in the water,
becoming stronger and
stronger, until water plants
and fish such as brook trout
can't live any longer. Acid rain

has damaged both the Washington Monument and Egypt's famous Sphinx, as well as many other buildings and monuments throughout the world by slowly eating away the stone.

If we do not stop releasing ozone-depleting chemicals, the protective ozone layer may not be able to recover. In places where the ozone layer is thin, more of the sun's harmful rays (radiation) reach

Sunbathers risk getting skin cancer from the sun's radiation.

the Earth. The result is that more people get skin cancer. Plants and animals also suffer.

If plankton (right) die, then other animals like the humpback whale (above) will not be able to survive.

Tiny ocean plants and animals called plankton cannot survive if they get too much radiation from the sun. Without plankton, many ocean animals would starve. The loss of the ozone layer can also lead to more bad ozone on ground level. Certain rays from the sun make smog worse. Without the good ozone layer above our planet, there would be more bad ozone down below.

Weather Worries

Air pollution may also cause
climate changes all over the
world. CFCs, methane, and
carbon dioxide are called
greenhouse gases. These
gases trap heat in the atmosphere the same way the glass
in a greenhouse holds the
sun's warmth inside. Without

greenhouse gases the Earth would be much colder. However, too much of a good thing may be causing trouble.

Since the late 1800s, average world temperatures have gone up by about 1°F. Snow and ice have melted in the Northern Hemisphere, which has made global sea levels rise between 4 and 10 inches (10 to 25 cm). Scientists cannot be sure that greenhouse gases alone are causing the Earth's

warming. They do know, however, that these gases trap heat
and that global temperatures
are rising.

What might the climate of
the future be like? Scientists
think temperatures will be
higher overall. Rainfall will be
heavier in some places; others
will dry out. The sea level is
expected to rise—up to 2 feet
(61 cm) along most of the U.S.
coast, sinking coastal lands.
Some plants and animals may

Floods may be more common in the future due to higher rainfall (above). The changing climate may lead to more hurricanes that do a lot of damage (right).

not be able to survive. Shifts in weather patterns may mean more bad weather and stronger hurricanes, typhoons, and tornadoes.

Measure the

Put an outdoor thermometer in a sunny spot for 15 minutes, then record the temperature. Next, place the thermometer inside a large, turned-over jar. The thermometer should fit completely inside the jar. Leave the thermometer in the jar in the same place as your first measurement for 15 minutes, then record the temperature again. The greenhouse effect causes the rise in temperature. In this case, the jar is the greenhouse, but greenhouse gases in the atmosphere do the same thing.

Greenhouse Effect

Put the thermometer in a jar to measure the greenhouse effect. ▼

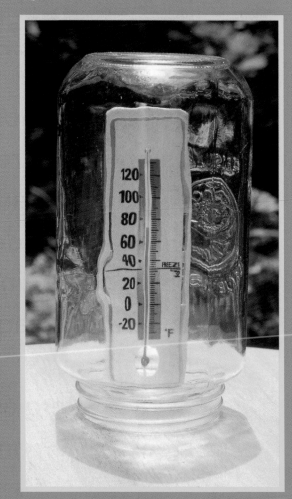

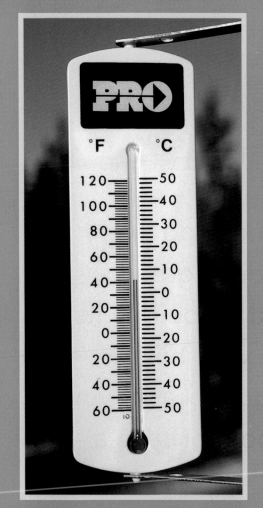

▲Take the temperature outdoors.

Help Clean Up the Air

Little things you can do every day can help reduce greenhouse gases and air pollutants.

•Walk or ride your bike instead of riding in a car. If you must drive, carpool or take a bus or train.

•Recycle glass, aluminum, steel, paper, and plastic.

Recycling is one way to
help clean up the air.

Donate old clothes and toys to charity. Buy things you need from thrift or second-hand stores. Everything you can reuse or recycle saves energy required to make new things.

•Turn off lights and appliances when you do not need them.

•Choose air-friendly energy suppliers if you have a choice. Some generate electricity using solar and wind

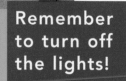

Remember to turn off the lights!

Wind power provides a clean source of energy.

power. These are clean energy sources that will never run out.

•Skip the power tools and use air-friendly push mowers and hand clippers for yard care.

•Plant trees and flowers. Plants are natural "air cleaners," removing carbon dioxide. Trees also provide shade, cutting cooling costs.

To Find Out More

To learn more about air pollution, check out these resources.

Books

Baines, John D. **Keeping the Air Clean.** Raintree Steck-Vaughn, 1998.

Kahl, Jonathan D.W. **Hazy Skies: Weather and the Environment.** Lerner Publications, 1997.

Miller, Christina G. **Air Alert: Rescuing the Earth's Atmosphere.** Atheneum, 1996.

Thompson, Colin. **Tower to the Sun.** Knopf, 1997.

Organizations and Online Sites

Environmental Protection Agency (EPA)
Public Information Center
401 M St., SW (TM-211B)
Washington, DC 20460
www.epa.gov/students

The EPA Student Center has information and activities about all environmental issues, including air pollution.

E Patrol
P.O. Box 30207
Kansas City, MO 64112
www.sprint.com/epatrol

Download a screen saver, play games, and learn more about saving energy.

Santa Barbara County Air Pollution Control District
26 Castilian Dr., B-23
Goleta, CA 93117
(805) 961-8800
www3.sbcapcd.org/student.htm

Check out a pollution simulator, print coloring pages, and learn about air pollution and how to prevent it.

The U.S. Department of Energy
1000 Independence Ave., SW
Washington, DC 20585
www.eren.doe.gov/kids.html

Learn about saving energy and new energy sources that are air friendly.

Important Words

acid rain water made when pollutants mix with water vapor in the atmosphere and come down in rain, snow, hail, sleet, or fog, harming plants, animals, and buildings

cancer a disease in which harmful growths spread in the body

fossil fuels fuels that are formed from the remains of ancient plants and animals and include coal, oil, and natural gas

ozone layer invisible gas in the atmosphere made of a type of oxygen that keeps some of the sun's harmful rays from reaching the Earth.

particulates tiny bits of stuff that float in the air and can cause breathing difficulty and disease

smog ozone at ground level that is a type of air pollution

Index

Meet the Author

Rhonda Lucas Donald has written for children and teachers for fifteen years. Her work has appeared in magazines such as *Ranger Rick* and *Your Big Backyard.* She specializes in writing about science and natural history and creating projects that make these subjects fun. Rhonda received the EdPress award for best newsletter of 1997 for *EarthSavers*, an environmental newspaper and activity guide. She has also written several other environmental True Books for Children's Press. She lives in North Carolina with her husband, Bruce, cats Sophie and Tory, and Maggie the dog.